HOMEMADE

Pies

fruit · cream · nut

KEEPERS AT HOME SAMPLER
· SEVEN ·

ISBN 1-890050-50-4

Text designed by Miriam Miller
Cover designed by Teresa Hochstetler

For additional copies or for a free catalog write:

2673 TR 421
Sugarcreek, OH 44681

Carlisle Press
WALNUT CREEK

TABLE OF CONTENTS

PIE-BAKING TIPS

> To make pie dough, you mix the shortening into the flour, often with a pastry cutter or fork, until crumbly. Add the liquid all at once and stir only until mixed.

> When baking pies, make a double recipe of dough and freeze the extra crusts, baked or unbaked for easy filling later.

> Fruit pies can be baked quickly for 15 min. at 425°. If the filling is precooked, thickened and hot.

> Test pie for doneness by giving the pan a quick twist to see whether the crust is loosened.

FRUIT PIES

APPLE PIE

1 c. brown sugar

    Boil, then add:

1 T. clear jel with a little water
$^1/_2$ tsp. salt
4 c. coarse shredded apples

1 c. water

1 tsp. ReaLemon
pinch of cinnamon

    Cool. Put in unbaked pie crust with another crust or crumbs. Bake at 450°.

DUTCH APPLE PIE

3 c. sliced apples
1 c. sugar
3 Tbsp. flour
$^1/_2$ tsp. cinnamon
1 beaten egg

1 tsp. vanilla
1 c. light cream
$^1/_2$ c. chopped nuts
1 Tbsp. butter
1 unbaked 9" shell

    Place apples in pie shell. Mix sugar, flour, and cinnamon. Combine egg, vanilla, and cream; add sugar mixture and mix well. Pour over apples. Sprinkle with nuts and dot with butter. Bake at 350° for 45–50 minutes, till apples are tender.

NO CRUST APPLE PIE

1 egg
$^1/_2$ c. white sugar
$^1/_2$ c. flour, sifted with baking
  powder and salt

1 tsp. baking powder
pinch of salt
2 med. apples, peeled, cored, and sliced
$^1/_2$ c. nuts

    Beat egg, then add the rest of the ingredients. Mix well and spread in a greased 9" pie plate. Bake at 350° for 30 minutes. Serve warm with ice cream.

STREUSEL APPLE PIE

1/2 c. white sugar
3 Tbsp. flour
3/4 tsp. cinnamon

1/4 tsp. nutmeg
1/4 tsp. salt
6 c. sliced apples

Toppings:
1 c. rolled oats
1/2 c. brown sugar
1/2 tsp. cinnamon

1/2 c. chopped pecans
1/3 c. butter, melted

Combine sugar, flour, cinnamon, nutmeg, and salt. Toss apples in sugar mixture. Pour into unbaked pie shell. Combine oats, sugar, cinnamon, nuts, and butter. Sprinkle over filling. Bake at 400° for 40 minutes, or until topping is brown and apples are tender.

SOUR CREAM APPLE PIE

2 eggs, beaten
3/4 c. white sugar
1 c. sour cream
2 Tbsp. flour

1 tsp. vanilla
1 tsp. apple pie spice
pinch of salt
2 c. sliced apples

Topping:
1/3 c. brown sugar
1/3 c. flour

1 tsp. apple pie spice
1/4 c. butter

Mix until crumbly. Bake at 350° for 30–40 minutes. Also delicious with sliced, fresh peaches instead of apples.

BERRY PIE

2/3 – 1 c. sugar
2 Tbsp. cornstarch or 4 Tbsp. flour
1/8 tsp. salt

3 c. fresh berries
1 Tbsp. butter

Mix sugar, cornstarch or flour, and salt; sprinkle over fruit in 9" pastry-lined pie pan. Dot with butter and adjust top crust. Bake in hot oven (450°) for 10 minutes, then moderate oven (350°) for about 30 minutes.

SUGARLESS APPLE PIE ♥

Apple pie is very easy to make using cider or apple juice concentrate (of course!) as the sweetener. We think it has much more flavor than apple pie with sugar! The filling can also be made in large batches and canned.

6 apples, peeled and sliced
¾ c. apple juice concentrate
⅓ c. water

1½ Tbsp. cornstarch
1 tsp. cinnamon
3 Tbsp. butter

Place apples and apple juice in saucepan. Bring to boil, reduce heat and simmer a few minutes. Dissolve cornstarch in water. Stir cornstarch mixture into apples. Bring to a boil and simmer just until apples begin to soften. Stir in cinnamon and butter. Pour into pie shell and cover with top crust. Bake at 350° for 45 minutes. For a crumb top, instead of a crust, mix ¾ c. flour and ⅓ c. butter. Spread evenly on pie before baking.

CANNED APPLE PIE FILLING

12 grated apples
5 c. white sugar

3 c. water
6 Tbsp. minute tapioca

Mix together. Process 15 minutes. Don't make jars too full. If using apples right away, cook 1 minute.

Topping for one pie:

1 c. quick rolled oats
⅓ c. chopped nuts
⅓ c. melted oleo

⅓ c. brown sugar
½ tsp. cinnamon

Mix and sprinkle on top of pie before baking. Put in baked pie shell and bake.

PEACH PIE #1

4¼ c. water
1½ c. sugar
3 oz. box peach jello

⅔ c. clear jel
pinch of salt
2 Tbsp. butter

Cook together. Then add 4 c. fresh peach slices. Bring to a boiling point. Makes 3 pies.

PEACH PIE #2

6 peaches, sliced
1 unbaked pie shell
1/4 c. flour

3/4 c. sugar
1 c. sweet cream

Arrange peaches in pie shell. Mix flour, sugar, and cream. Pour over peaches. Top with crumbs.

Topping:

1/3 c. flour
1/3 c. sugar

3 Tbsp. butter

Combine and put over first mixture. Bake at 425° for 10 minutes. Lower heat to 350° and bake until custard is set (approx. 30 minutes).

PEACH AND PRALINE PIE ❤

3 Tbsp. whole wheat flour
1/4 tsp. salt
1/2 c. maple syrup

1/4 tsp. nutmeg
3 eggs

Combine and beat together well.
Stir in:

3 c. fresh peaches, cubed and peeled
   or canned peaches, drained and cubed

1/4 c. butter, melted

Pour into pastry-lined pan.
Combine:

1/2 c. pecans, chopped
1/3 c. wheat flour

2 Tbsp. honey
2 Tbsp. soft butter

Sprinkle over top of filling. Bake at 400° for 35–45 minutes or until center is set.

STRAWBERRY PIE #1

3/4 c. sugar
1 1/2 c. water

1 Tbsp. cornstarch

Boil for 3 minutes. Stir in one small box strawberry jello. Let cool, but not set. Put 1 qt. fresh berries in baked pie shell. Pour cooled sauce over berries. Refrigerate for a couple hours. Top with Cool Whip and serve.

STRAWBERRY CREAM PIE ❤

1 baked pie shell
1 c. yogurt, drained
8 oz. cream cheese

1/4 c. honey
1 tsp. vanilla
2 c. sliced or cooked strawberries,
   sweetened

Combine yogurt, cream cheese, honey, and vanilla. Beat to the consistency of whipped cream. Pour into baked pie shell and refrigerate until set. Before serving, top with strawberries.

Or: Fold strawberries into cream pie before pouring into baked pie shell. Then pour into pie shell and refrigerate until set.

Variation: Use peaches, blueberries, or other sliced fruit instead of strawberries.

STRAWBERRY PIE #2

5 cans Eagle Brand milk
4 lb. frozen strawberries, sweetened

2 lg. tubs Cool Whip

Cook Eagle Brand milk in water for 1 hour. Stir all together and put in pie crusts. Will make 9 pies. Note: To cook Eagle Brand milk, be sure to remove all labels and keep cans completely covered with water during cooking time. Because of the heat, cans could explode if not covered with water.

BLUEBERRY PIE

2 1/2 c. blueberries
1 c. sugar
1/4 c. flour

1 Tbsp. lemon juice
2 Tbsp. butter
1/8 tsp. salt

Combine blueberries, sugar, flour, salt, and lemon juice. Fill 8-inch pastry-lined pie pan. Dot with butter and adjust top crust. Bake in hot oven (450°) for 10 minutes, then in moderate oven (350°) for about 30 minutes.

SOUR CHERRY PIE

1 qt. sour cherries
1 qt. water
2 c. white sugar

¹/₂ tsp. cherry flavor
pinch of salt
red food color

Thicken with:

4 Tbsp. clear jel (heaping)

¹/₄ c. white sugar

Moisten with water. Heat the first ingredients to boiling. Then add the last two. Makes 3 pies.

GROUND CHERRY PIE

1¹/₂ –2 c. ground cherries
1¹/₄ c. brown sugar
pinch of salt

1 Tbsp. ReaLemon juice or vinegar
1 Tbsp. butter

Put cherries in saucepan. Add enough water to cover berries. Add ReaLemon juice, brown sugar, and salt. Bring to a boil. Thicken with clear jel. Turn down heat and boil for 2 minutes. Take off stove and add butter. Pour into unbaked pie shell. Put crust on top and bake at 450° until golden brown.

RHUBARB CREAM PIE

³/₄ c. rhubarb
³/₄ c. sugar
1 c. water
pinch of soda
1 c. milk

1 egg
2 Tbsp. cornstarch
1 Tbsp. butter
1 tsp. vanilla

Boil first 4 ingredients together for 10 minutes. Mix together next 3 ingredients; add to boiled mixture and stir. Bring to a boil. Take off heat and add butter and vanilla. Pour into baked pie shell. Top with Cool Whip when cool.

RHUBARB PIE

2 c. rhubarb, cut fine
1 egg, beaten
1 tsp. vanilla

2 Tbsp. flour
1 c. sugar

Mix above ingredients and place in unbaked pie shell.
Crumb Mixture:

¹/₃ c. butter
³/₄ c. flour

¹/₂ c. brown sugar

Sprinkle crumb mixture on top of rhubarb. Bake at 425° for 5 minutes, then at 350° for 30 minutes.

RHUBARB DELIGHT

1¹/₂ c. rhubarb
1 c. sugar
¹/₄ c. water

3 oz. strawberry Jell-O
1 c. Rich's topping
1 tsp. vanilla

Simmer first 3 ingredients together until rhubarb is tender. Stir in Jell-O until dissolved. Cool until partly set. Whip Rich's topping and vanilla. Fold in cream mixture. Pour into baked pie shell.

BLACKBERRY CUSTARD PIE

1 c. flour
3 eggs (beat whites)
3 c. milk
¹/₂ qt. blackberries or other fruit to each pie

1 c. honey
pinch of salt
¹/, tsp. cinnamon

Fold in beaten egg whites last. Sprinkle cinnamon on top. Pour into unbaked pie shell. Bake at 350° for 20–30 minutes. Makes 2 pies.

PINEAPPLE SPONGE PIE

1 c. sugar
3 egg yolks
1 c. milk
1½ Tbsp. flour

2 Tbsp. butter
¾ c. crushed pineapple, drained
3 egg whites, beaten
½ tsp. salt

Mix all together, adding beaten egg whites last. Bake at 425° for 8 minutes, then reduce temperature to 325° and bake 30–35 minutes longer. Makes 1 pie.

ELDERBERRY CUSTARD PIE

1 c. elderberry juice
4 Tbsp. flour
1 c. sugar

¼ tsp. salt
1 egg, separated
1 c. milk

Bring juice to a boil. Combine flour, sugar and salt. Gradually add the egg yolk and milk. Add this mixture to the boiling juice and stir till thickened. Fold in stiffly beaten egg whites. Pour into unbaked pie shell. Bake at 350° for 20–30 minutes.

GRANDPA'S RAISIN CRUMB PIE

¾ c. raisins
2 c. water
1 c. brown sugar

1 Tbsp. vinegar
salt

Boil all ingredients. Thicken with 2 Tbsp. cornstarch. Pour into baked crust. Crumbs:

1 c. flour
¼ c. shortening

½ c. brown sugar
½ tsp. salt

Bake at 350° until browned.

SOUR CREAM RAISIN PIE

3 eggs
1 c. sugar
1½ c. sour cream

3 Tbsp. cornstarch
1 c. milk
¾ c. boiled raisins, drained

Beat egg yolks only. Mix with milk, sugar, and cornstarch. Stir over medium heat until thick. Add boiled, drained raisins. Fold in sour cream. Pour mixture into baked pie crust. Top with meringue or whipped cream. Makes one small pie.

RAISIN CREAM PIE

1 c. cooked raisins
2 c. milk
½ c. brown sugar
½ c. white sugar

2 egg yolks, beaten
6 Tbsp. flour
1 Tbsp. butter

Cook until thick. Last add raisins and butter. Put in a baked pie crust. Top with Cool Whip.

MOCK MINCE PIE

3 c. bread crumbs
3 c. white sugar
½ c. butter
½ c. vinegar
1 c. raisins

1 tsp. cloves
1 tsp. allspice
1 tsp. nutmeg
3 c. water

Mix all together. Makes 4 pies.

MINCE PIES

6 c. apples
1 pt. hamburger
1 c. raisins
3 Tbsp. vinegar
1 Tbsp. butter, melted

2 c. sugar
1 tsp. cinnamon
1 tsp. allspice
salt to taste

Mix all ingredients, then pour into 2 unbaked pie shells. Bake at 350° for 25–35 minutes.

CREAM PIES

SUGARLESS PUMPKIN PIE 💙

4 c. pumpkin
3 Tbsp. flour
2 eggs
1 tsp. salt

1 pt. milk
1 Tbsp. cinnamon
1 c. cider concentrate

Mix all together and pour into two unbaked pie shells. Bake at 350° for 45 minutes. To make sweeter pies, add more concentrate and cut back on milk.

PUMPKIN PIE #1

4 eggs, separated
1 c. white sugar
1 c. brown sugar
2 c. pumpkin
2 tsp. pumkin pie spice

4 Tbsp. flour
pinch of salt
2 tsp. vanilla
5 c. milk (I use 1-2 cans Pet milk) -heat

Beat egg whites, then beat egg yolks and brown sugar together until light in color. Add white sugar, then rest of the ingredients. Fold in egg whites last. Bake at 425° until brown. Yield: 2 pies.

PUMPKIN PIE #2 ❤

4 eggs, separated
2 c. mashed pumpkin
¼ c. wheat flour
½ tsp. pumpkin pie spice

3 c. milk
½ c. honey
½ c. sorghum

Mix all ingredients except egg whites, beating thoroughly. Fold in stiffly beaten egg whites. Pour into 2 unbaked pie crusts. Bake in moderate oven until nicely browned and done.

IMPOSSIBLE PUMPKIN PIE ❤ (FORMS ITS OWN CRUST)

¼ c. butter, melted
½ c. honey or sorghum
1½ c. pumpkin
½ c. wheat flour
½ tsp. cinnamon

2 eggs
½ tsp. salt
¼ tsp. ginger
¼ tsp. nutmeg
1½ c. milk

Separate eggs. Put yolks in large bowl and add other ingredients, beating well. Beat egg whites and fold in last. Pour into pie pan. Bake at 425° for 15 minutes, then at 350° for 45 minutes or until filling is set.

VELVET CUSTARD PIE

Soak 1½ envelopes gelatin. Heat 6 c. milk to scalding. Add gelatin and the following:

6 egg yolks
½ c. white sugar or to suit taste

1 c. brown sugar
vanilla

Beat egg whites and add last. This makes 2 large pies. Bake like other custard pies.

CUSTARD PIE

¾ c. brown sugar
2 egg yolks

2 rounded Tbsp. flour
½ tsp. salt

Mix sugar, flour, eggs, salt, and a little milk. Stir until thoroughly mixed, then add 1¾ c. milk. Beat egg whites and fold in. Bake at 425° for 15 minutes, then at 350° until it's a nice dark brown– approximately 15 minutes, or until the middle of the pie is still a little shaky when touched.

SPONGE LEMON PIE

1 c. sugar (scant)
1 Tbsp. flour
1 lemon

2 egg yolks
1 c. milk

Grated rind and juice of 1 lemon. Beat whites of two eggs stiffly and stir in last. Bake slowly at 325° for 45–60 minutes until knife inserted in center comes out clean.

FAMOUS LEMON PIE

3 Tbsp. cornstarch
1¼ c. sugar
¼ c. lemon juice
1 Tbsp. grated lemon rind

3 eggs, separated
1½ c. boiling water
1- 9" baked pie shell
½ tube soft cream cheese, opt.

Combine cornstarch, sugar, lemon juice, and lemon rind. Beat egg yolks. Add to cornstarch mixture. Gradually add boiling water. Heat to boiling over direct heat, then boil gently for 4 minutes, stirring constantly. After cooled, add cream cheese. Pour into pie shell. Top with Rich's topping.

CHOCOLATE CHIFFON PIE

1 Tbsp. gelatin
1/4 c. cold water
1/2 c. white sugar
2 Tbsp. cocoa
1/2 c. hot milk

1/2 c. light coffee
1/2 tsp. salt
1 tsp. vanilla
1 c. whipped cream
chopped nuts for top

Soak gelatin in cold water for 5 minutes. Boil sugar, cocoa, hot milk, coffee, and salt. Add gelatin to this mixture, stirring thoroughly. Allow to cool. Add vanilla as mixture begins to thicken. Fold in whipped cream. Put in baked pie shell and top with nuts. Makes 1 large pie.

CAROB PIE ♥

1 c. raw cashews or almonds
1/4 c. cornstarch
1/4 c. dates

1/2 c. carob powder
1/2 tsp. salt
1/2 tsp. vanilla

Put all ingredients in blender, then add enough water to make 4 c. of liquid. Blend until smooth. Pour into pan and cook over medium heat, stirring occasionally, until mixture thickens. Pour into baked pie shell. Chill. Sprinkle coconut on top before serving.

CHOCOLATE MOCHA PIE

Dissolve 1 Tbsp. gelatin in 1/4 c. cold water. Combine in saucepan:

1 Tbsp. cocoa
1 tsp. coffee
1/8 tsp. salt
1 tsp. vanilla

3/4 c. sugar
1 1/4 c. milk
1 c. cream

Bring to a boil, stirring constantly. Remove from heat and add gelatin. Cool till slightly thickened. Beat the cooked mixture until smooth. Beat cream. Add vanilla. Fold whipped cream into cooked mixture. Pour into 9" baked pie shell and top with nuts.

GRANDMA'S CHOCOLATE PIE

4 egg yolks
3 tsp. cocoa
1¼ c. milk

1½ c. sugar, divided
2 Tbsp. flour
1 tsp. vanilla

Beat egg yolks with 1 c. sugar. Mix cocoa, flour, and remaining sugar together, then add milk. Add this mixture to the egg mixture and cook until thickened, stirring continually. Add vanilla and pour into unbaked pie shell. Bake at 375° for 30–35 minutes. Beat egg whites, gradually adding 4 Tbsp. sugar until stiff peaks form. Place this meringue on top of cooked pie and return to oven for 5 minutes. Delicious! (Similar to a lemon meringue pie.)

BUTTERSCOTCH PIE

1 c. brown sugar

2 Tbsp. milk

Cook 6 minutes.
Add:

1½ c. rich milk
1 egg

2 Tbsp. flour
1 Tbsp. butter

Put in a baked pie crust and cool.

CARAMEL PIE

1 c. brown sugar
1½ c. sweet milk
2 Tbsp. flour

1 egg
1 tsp. vanilla

Mix all together and cook in a double boiler until thick.

PEANUT BUTTER PIE #1

Crumbs:

⅓ c. peanut butter
¾ c. powdered sugar

pinch of salt

Blend together until mealy. Sprinkle ⅓ of crumbs over pie shell.
Combine:

2 c. milk
½ c. white sugar

⅓ c. flour
3 egg yolks

Heat milk; mix rest of ingredients and mix. Stir into hot milk; bring to a boil. Remove from heat and add 1 Tbsp. butter and 1 tsp. vanilla. Cool; pour into pie shell. Top with beaten egg whites or whipped topping. Sprinkle with the rest of crumbs on top.

PEANUT BUTTER PIE #2

8 oz. cream cheese (stir until creamy)
¾ c. peanut butter
1 tsp. vanilla

8 oz. Eagle Brand milk
3 Tbsp. ReaLemon
1 c. whipped topping

Mix together and put in baked pie shell.

COCONUT CREAM PIE #1 ❤

1 baked pie shell
8 oz. cream cheese
1 c. yogurt

3 Tbsp. honey
2 tsp. vanilla
1¼ c. shredded unsweetened coconut

Blend together yogurt, cream cheese, honey, and vanilla. Fold in coconut, reserving a little for topping. Pour into pie shell. Top with remaining coconut and chill until set.

COCONUT CREAM PIE #2

½ c. brown sugar
½ c. white sugar
2 egg yolks
½ tsp. vanilla

⅓ c. butter
1 Tbsp. flour
1 c. milk
1 c. shredded coconut

Heat milk. Mix sugar, flour, and egg yolks with a little milk. Add to heated milk. Bring to a boil. Remove from heat; add coconut, butter, and vanilla. Pour into a baked pie shell.

CREAM CHEESE FILLING FOR PIE

4 oz. cream cheese
1 Tbsp. milk

1 Tbsp. sugar
1½ c. Cool Whip

Mix cream cheese, milk, and sugar with wire whisk until well mixed. Gently stir in Cool Whip. Put this in bottom of baked pie shell and top with your favorite fruit.

MARSHMALLOW PIE

20 marshmallows
½ c. milk

1 c. whipped cream
½ c. ground sweet chocolate

Heat marshmallows and milk in double boiler until marshmallows are melted. Cool. Fill a baked pie crust. Sprinkle top with chocolate.

COCONUT MACAROON PIE

¾ c. white sugar
¾ c. brown sugar
½ c. oleo, softened
2 eggs

⅓ c. flour
2 c. milk
1½ c. coconut

Beat together sugar and eggs. Add oleo and flour; blend well. Add milk. Fold in 1 c. coconut. Pour into unbaked pie shell. Top with ½ c. coconut. Bake at 300° for 1 hour. A double batch makes 3 pies.

CREAM CHEESE PIE ❤

1 baked pie shell
1½ Tbsp. unflavored gelatin
¼ c. cold water
2 eggs, beaten
¼ c. milk

8 oz. cream cheese
1 c. yogurt
⅓ c. honey
2 tsp. vanilla

Mix gelatin and water and heat until gelatin dissolves. Blend eggs with milk and add to gelatin. Stirring constantly, cook over low heat until mixture coats a silver spoon. Cool. Cream honey, cheese, and vanilla. Add yogurt and continue mixing until smooth. Slowly stir in cold gelatin mixture. Chill a little more, then beat until creamy smooth. Pour into a nut or coconut pie shell. Refrigerate to set.

EGGNOG PIE

1 tsp. gelatin
1 Tbsp. cold water
1 c. milk
½ c. white sugar
2 Tbsp. cornstarch

½ tsp. salt
3 egg yolks, beaten
1 Tbsp. butter
1 Tbsp. vanilla
1 c. whipped cream

Soak gelatin in cold water. Scald milk. Combine sugar, cornstarch, and salt; mix well. Add to milk and cook until thick. Add eggs and cook a little longer. Add butter, vanilla, and gelatin. Cool, then fold in whipped cream and pour into baked pie shell.

NUT & OATMEAL PIES

PECAN PIES #1

3 eggs, slightly beaten
$^1/_2$ c. brown sugar
1 c. light corn syrup
  (with a little water added)
1 Tbsp. flour

1 Tbsp. butter, melted
$^1/_2$ tsp. salt
1 c. pecans or walnuts
1 tsp. vanilla

   Mix all together and add 1 c. pecans or walnuts last. Put in unbaked pie crust and bake as you would for custard pie. Bake about 45 minutes.

PECAN PIES #2

3 eggs, beaten
$^3/_4$ c. brown & white sugar (half & half)
$^1/_2$ Tbsp. flour
$^3/_4$ c. Karo ($^1/_2$ light and $^1/_2$ dark)
1 Tbsp. butter

$^1/_4$ c. water
$^1/_4$ c. rolled oats
pinch of salt
1 tsp. vanilla
$^1/_2$ c. chopped nuts

   Beat eggs and add remaining ingredients. Bake at 350° in unbaked pie shell till top is firm.

SURPRISE PECAN PIE

$^1/_4$ c. margarine, softened
1 c. sugar
3 eggs
$^3/_4$ c. light corn syrup

$^1/_4$ tsp. salt
1 tsp. vanilla
$^1/_2$ c. chocolate chips
$^1/_2$ c. chopped pecans

   Cream margarine and sugar. Add eggs, corn syrup, salt, and vanilla. Stir. Add chips and nuts and stir well. Pour into a 9" pie crust. Bake at 375° for 40–45 minutes. Allow time to set before serving.

HONEY PIE ❤

1 c. honey
4 beaten eggs
1 c. chopped almonds
1- 9" pie shell, unbaked

dash of nutmeg
dash of cinnamon
4 Tbsp. butter
2 tsp. vanilla

In a saucepan, bring honey to a boil. Add beaten eggs, stirring constantly with a fork. Add butter, vanilla, almonds, cinnamon, and nutmeg. Pour into pie shell and bake at 350° for 20 minutes or until filling is set.

DOUBLE PEANUT PIE

2 eggs
1/3 c. creamy peanut butter
1/3 c. sugar
1/3 c. light corn syrup
1/3 c. butter or oleo, melted

1/3 c. dark corn syrup
1 tsp. vanilla
1 c. salted peanuts
1- 9" unbaked pastry shell
whipped cream or ice cream

Mix and pour into the crust. Bake at 375° for 30–35 minutes, or until set. Cool; serve with whipped cream or ice cream if desired.

OATMEAL NUT PIE

2 eggs, beaten
2/3 c. oatmeal (quick)
2/3 c. white sugar
2/3 c. nuts
1/2 c. milk

1 tsp. vanilla
2 tsp. oleo
1/2 c. brown sugar
1/2 c. light Karo

Beat eggs. Add rest of ingredients. Pour into an unbaked pie shell. Bake at 375°.

OATMEAL PIE ❤

3 eggs, beaten
1/3 c. honey
1/2 c. molasses
2 Tbsp. browned butter
1/2 tsp. maple flavoring

1/4 c. quick oats
1/2 c. coconut
3/4 –1 c. milk
1 tsp. vanilla
1/4 tsp. cinnamon

Blend together. Pour into unbaked pie shell. Bake for 30–35 minutes at 350°.

MAPLE NUT PIE

Heat 1/2 c. milk and 1 c. maple syrup. Add 2 slightly beaten egg yolks. Cook a little, then add 1 Tbsp. gelatin, softened in a little cold water. Add 1 tsp. maple flavoring. Chill until mixture begins to thicken. Add 2 stiffly beaten egg whites. Add 1 c. whipped cream and 1/2 c. chopped nut meats. Pour into pie shell. If you double this recipe it makes three 8" pies.

HICKORY NUT PIE

3 c. white sugar
2 1/4 c. light Karo
5 Tbsp. flour
1 c. cold water

5 Tbsp. butter, melted
2 1/2 c. hickory nuts
10 eggs

Beat eggs. Add remaining ingredients. Pour into unbaked pie shell. Bake at 350° for 40 minutes. Makes 3 large pies.

MISCELLANEOUS PIES

BOB ANDY PIE

2 c. sugar
3 Tbsp. flour
1/2 tsp. cream of tartar

1 tsp. cinnamon
3 eggs
butter, size of an egg

Mix dry ingredients; add butter and eggs. Beat; add 3 c. milk. Put into an unbaked pie crust and bake in a hot oven.

GRAPE NUT PIE

1/2 c. Grape Nuts
1/2 c. lukewarm water
1 c. brown sugar
1 c. light Karo

1/4 c. butter
1/8 tsp. salt
3 eggs
1 tsp. vanilla

Soak Grape Nuts in warm water until water is absorbed. Combine sugar, Karo, butter, and salt in saucepan. Quickly bring to a boil and remove from heat. Beat eggs until foamy. Add a small amount of hot syrup mixture to eggs, beating well. Add rest of syrup and mix well. Stir in Grape Nuts and vanilla. Bake in pastry shell at 375° for about 30 minutes. Makes 1 pie.

SHOO-FLY PIE

Mix together until crumbly:
2 c. flour
1 1/2 c. brown sugar

1/2 c. shortening

Take out 2 c. crumbs for top of pie. To remainder of crumbs, add 2 beaten eggs, 2 c. molasses (we use 1 1/2 c. light Karo and 1/2 c. blackstrap molasses), and 1 1/2 c. hot water (not boiling). Mix well. Dissolve 2 tsp. baking soda in 1/2 c. hot water and add. Now put into pie shells and top with crumbs. Bake at 450° for 10 minutes. Reduce heat to 375° and bake for 30 minutes, or until top is dry and done. Makes 2 lg. pies.

VANILLA CRUMB PIE

½ c. brown sugar (packed)
1 Tbsp. flour
¼ c. light Karo

1½ tsp. vanilla
1 c. water
1 egg, beaten

Cook this over medium heat, stirring until mixture comes to a boil. Let cool.

1 c. flour
½ c. brown sugar (packed)
½ tsp. cream of tartar

½ tsp. soda
⅛ tsp. salt
¼ c. butter

Mix this until crumbly. Pour cooled mixture into pie shell. Top with crumbs. Bake at 350° for 40 minutes or until golden brown.

VANILLA TART PIE

1 c. sugar
1 c. molasses
1 tsp. vanilla

2 c. water
1 egg

Mix together and pour into 4 unbaked pie crusts.
Topping:

3 c. flour
2 c. sugar
1 egg

1 tsp. baking soda
½ c. lard
1 c. buttermilk

Mix and spoon on top of first part. Bake at 375° till set.

UNION PIE

1 c. sour cream
1 c. sour milk
1 c. white sugar
1 c. maple-flavored Karo
2 eggs, beaten

3 Tbsp. flour
½ tsp. soda
1 tsp. cinnamon
1 tsp. nutmeg

Mix together. Bake in 2 unbaked crusts at 325° for 40 minutes or until done.

RITZ CRACKER PIE

Beat 3 egg whites until stiff, adding 1 c. sugar gradually. Fold in 1 tsp. baking powder, 1 c. pecans, and crumbs of 24 Ritz crackers. Add 1 tsp. vanilla. Bake in buttered pan at 350° for 25 minutes. Top with your favorite fruit and whipped topping.

RICE KRISPIE PIE

Beat 2 eggs.
Add:

2/3 c. sugar
1/2 c. Karo
1/4 tsp. salt

3 Tbsp. melted butter
1/2 c. water
1 c. Rice Krispies

Pour into unbaked pie shell. Bake at 400° for 10–15 minutes, then turn back to 300°.

SWEET YAM PIE (NO SUGAR)

Use your favorite crust. Preheat oven to 325°. Blend all ingredients (except 3 egg whites) until very smooth. Use a potato masher or blender.

4 cooked, mashed yams
1/4 c. honey
3 Tbsp. butter
1 Tbsp. cinnamon
1/2 tsp. salt

1/2 c. orange juice
1/4 c. maple syrup
3 egg yolks
1/2 tsp. vanilla

Beat the 3 egg whites and a pinch of cream of tartar till stiff peaks form. Fold this into the batter and pour into pie shell. Garnish, if desired, with pecan halves, bake for 40 minutes until set.

TREASURE CHEST ICE CREAM PIE

2 c. Rice Krispies (slightly crushed)
1/2 c. brown sugar
1/3 c. melted butter or oleo

1/2 c. chopped nuts
1/2 c. coconut
1 qt. vanilla ice cream, softened

Mix together Rice Krispies, nuts, and coconut, and brown in the oven. Stir in sugar and margarine. Put half in 9" x 9" pan. Spoon in the ice cream and put other half of crumbs on top. Freeze. You can also line pie pans with crust and make like a pie.

SNITZ PIES

1 quart dried apple snitz boiled in 1 1/2 c. water until soft, and no water remains. Put through colander and add:

1 qt. applesauce
1 1/2 c. brown sugar

1/2 tsp. cinnamon
1/2 tsp. salt

Make pie dough, then shape dough to the size of a large egg. Roll out thin as pie dough. Fold over to make a crease through center, Fold back and make 2 holes in top part of the dough. On the other half, place 1/2 c. of the filling. Wet edges and fold over. Press edges together. Cut off remaining dough with pie crimper. Brush top with buttermilk or beaten egg. Bake at 450° until brown.

FRY PIES

Dough:
10 c. cake flour
2 c. water

3 c. Creamtex or Hyscore shortening
1 Tbsp. salt

Glaze:
2 lb. powdered sugar
1/3 c. cornstarch
1/4 c. milk

1 tsp. vanilla
water as needed

Roll out dough very thin. If you don't have a fry pie maker, use the lid of a Lifetime coffee pot for the cutter. Put a spoonful of pie filling on the cut out circles; wet the edges. Fold over to make a half-moon pie. Seal the edges by pressing with a fork. Deep fry in Creamtex or Hyscore shortening. Dip in glaze while pies are still warm. Lay on a rack to dry. (Have your pie filling a little extra thick.)

CRUSTS

DELICIOUS WHOLE WHEAT PASTRY CRUST ❤

2 c. whole wheat pastry flour, sifted
1 tsp. salt
¾ c. butter (scant)

4–5 Tbsp. ice water
2 Tbsp. wheat germ

Sift flour and salt. Add wheat germ. With pastry cutter, blend in butter. Sprinkle ice water over mixture and blend with fork. Pastry should be just moist enough to hold together.

PIE CRUST #1

3 c. flour
1 c. shortening
1 tsp. salt
2 eggs, beaten
1 tsp. vinegar
water to make ¾ c. liquid

PIE CRUST #2

1½ c. wheat flour
1 Tbsp. cornmeal
6 Tbsp. butter
⅓ c. ice water
honey
salt

PIE CRUST MIX

9 lb. flour
3½ lb. lard
1 c. cornstarch

2 Tbsp. baking powder
1 Tbsp. salt
2 c. brown sugar

Store in cool place or refrigerator. To prepare crust, add ¼ c. milk to 1½ c. mix. Work until smooth; roll out and place in 9" pie pan. Water may be substituted for milk. Whole wheat flour can also be used, but I added more shortening for a smooth texture.

NEVER FAIL PIE DOUGH MIX

5 lb. bag of Gold Medal flour
3 lb. can of butter-flavored Crisco

½ c. white sugar
2 Tbsp. salt

Mix with hands and put in a Fix 'n' Mix bowl. Place in cool pantry or on basement floor. 1 c. mix will make 1 crust. Add water till right consistency. Delicious to use for apple dumplings!

PIE DOUGH ❤

2½ c. wheat flour
1 tsp. baking powder
1 Tbsp. vinegar
¼ c. water

½ c. cream, or as needed
½ tsp. salt
½ c. butter
1 egg

Makes 4- 1 crust pies.

PERFECT PIE DOUGH

2¼ c. lard
2 tsp. baking powder
1 Tbsp. vinegar

1½ tsp. salt
6 c. flour

Put 1 Tbsp. vinegar in 1 c. and fill up with hot water. Pour over lard and let stand until soft. Stir in flour (part whole wheat if you wish). Set in cold place overnight. Enough for approximately 6 pies.

OATMEAL PIE CRUST

1 c. rolled oats
⅓ c. sifted flour

⅓ c. brown sugar
¼ tsp. salt

Combine the above ingredients, then cut in ⅓ c. butter till crumbly. Grease pie pan. Press crumbs on bottom and sides of pie pan. Bake at 350° for 15 minutes or till light brown. Substitute option for flour and sugar: Use ¾ c. flour and ⅓ c. honey.

RICE PIE CRUST

¾ c. butter
1½ c. rice flour

1 Tbsp. water
1 egg

Mix all ingredients together well. Roll between waxed paper and fit into pie plate. Bake at 350° for 8–10 minutes.
Note: This pie crust must be baked first before filling it.

COCONUT PIE SHELL

1½ c. unsweetened coconut

2½ Tbsp. butter

Mix and pat into pie pan. Bake in 350° oven until edges brown. Cool before filling.

KEEPERS AT HOME

A quarterly Magazine for "Mothers at Home."

Keepers at Home is a quarterly magazine especially for Christian mothers and homemakers. Each issue is packed with ideas, encouragement, and how-to articles on anything from how to better organize your home to making your own noodles! Practical as well as spiritual insights are shared by writers and readers. Regular features include: **Gleanings From Gramma** (spiritual lessons on a relevant subject), **My End of the Hoe** (our garden editor shares on a gardening subject), **Gracia's Garden** (how-to on herbs), **Care to Share** (readers' questions–

readers' responses), **Birth Announcements, Recipes** (centerfold tear-out of readers' recipes on a specific food category).

If you're a mother there are many reasons why you'd enjoy Keepers at Home. Order your own subscriptions today! Also makes a perfect gift!

1 year (4 issues): $12; 2 years (8 issues): $22; Sample Copy: $3

For a complete list of Carlisle Press products, request a FREE catalog!

To order, call or write:

2673 TR 421
Sugarcreek, OH 44681
1-800-852-4482

Carlisle Press
WALNUT CREEK

Here's More
Sampler Series Titles

5¹/₂" x 8¹/₂" · 32 pp · **$3.99 each**

Homemade Breads

Homemade Cereals

Homemade Salad Dress

Hot & Hearty Soups

Homemade Pizzas

Want a complete set?

Get all 8 books packaged with a gift ribbon for only $2.37 each (save $12.93)
Complete set of 8 in a Gift Set **$18.99**

Healthful Cookies

Homemade Ice Cream